ONSTAGE/BACKSTAGE

ONSTAGE
BACKSTAGE

by Caryn Huberman and JoAnne Wetzel

Carolrhoda Books, Inc. • Minneapolis

This book would not have been possible without the help of Patricia Briggs, director of the Palo Alto Children's Theatre. The authors would like to thank Pat and her staff—Jim Wallis, Alison Williams, Linda Stubo, and assistant director Michael Litfin—for sharing their professional knowledge. Wilson Graham, Jr., was a great help in sharing his expertise in theater photography with us. The cast and crew of *Just So Stories* were wonderful. Thank you for letting us be a part of your show.

Copyright © 1987 by Caryn Huberman and JoAnne Wetzel

LIBRARY OF CONGRESS CATALOGING-IN-PUBLICATION DATA

Huberman, Caryn.
    Onstage/backstage.

    Summary: A ten-year-old actress tells about her association with the Palo Alto Children's Theatre, the oldest children's theater in the United States, and her performance in their staging of Kipling's "Just So Stories."
    1. Geisler, Chessa—Performances—Juvenile literature. 2. Palo Alto Children's Theatre—Juvenile literature. 3. Children's plays—Presentation, etc.—California—Palo Alto—Juvenile literature. 4. Children as actors—California—Palo Alto—Juvenile literature. 5. Kipling, Rudyard, 1865-1936. Just so stories—Juvenile literature. 6. Kipling, Rudyard, 1865-1936—Adaptations—Juvenile literature. 7. Actors—United States—Biography—Juvenile literature. [1. Theater—Production and direction. 2. Acting. 3. Children as actors. 4. Palo Alto Childrens Theatre. 5. Geisler, Chessa. 6. Children's plays—Presentations, etc. 7. Kipling, Rudyard, 1865-1936. Just so stories. 8. Kipling, Rudyard, 1865-1936—Adaptations] I. Wetzel, JoAnne. II. Title.
PN2287.G45H83   1987   792'.028'0924   87-11599
ISBN 0-87614-307-9 (lib. bdg.)

Manufactured in the United States of America

1 2 3 4 5 6 7 8 9 10 97 96 95 94 93 92 91 90 89 88 87

*To Jill, Lara, and Andrew, who are a part of the happy
tradition, and to Bernardo and Gary for their applause*

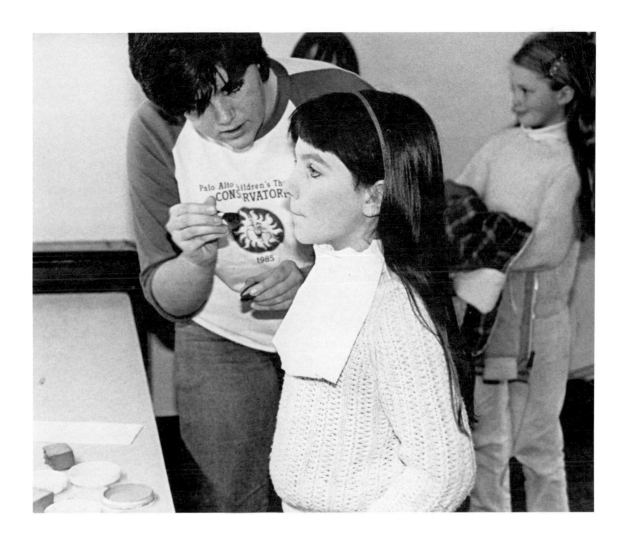

My name is Chessa Geisler. I'm 10 years old, and
I love to act. I'm playing the part of Pingle the 'Stute
Fish in a play based on Rudyard Kipling's *Just So
Stories*, and tonight is opening night. This is the third
play I've been in, but I've never had a part this big
before. I have 15 lines.

My play is being performed at the Palo Alto
Children's Theatre in Palo Alto, California. It's the
oldest children's theater in the United States where
all of the acting is done by children. We do a lot
of the backstage work, too.

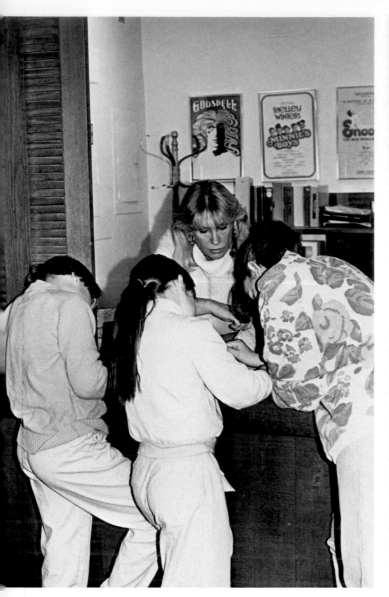 

My friend Shannon and I tried out for the play together. She'd never tried out for a play before, so I showed her what to do when we got to the theater. Linda Stubo, the program assistant, gave us audition cards. We had to write down a lot of information on our cards including our names, ages, and heights. Shannon is 4 feet 7 inches, and I'm 4 feet 5 inches.

After we finished filling out our cards, we took them
to Patricia Briggs. Pat is the director of the Palo Alto
Children's Theatre. She directed me in the other two
plays I was in. Pat told us to sit with everyone else in the
front of the house (the house is the part of the theater
where the audience sits). I was pretty nervous about
getting a part since hundreds of kids were trying out.

Pat told us to go onstage and line up by height.
Then she counted us off into groups of 10. Each group
took turns reading lines from the play. I tried to read
as loudly as I could and with lots of expression.

Next we had to do improvisations about animals. Improvisation means that we act out something without rehearsing it beforehand. My group's improv (that's short for improvisation) was about some ducks walking to a duckpond. We all laughed as we watched each other waddling around. After Pat saw the improvs, she said that some of us would be called back for a second audition. She said that she wished there were enough parts in the play for all of us because we were all very good.

The next day after school, I waited by the telephone while I did my homework. I wanted to get called back so badly. The wait seemed like forever, but when she finally called two days later, Linda said, "Come to callbacks Saturday at ten o'clock." Saturday seemed like a long way away!

When I went to callbacks, I did another reading and another improv. The waiting after that was even worse than it had been the first time, but finally Linda called and told me that I'd gotten a part in the play. I was so excited. I wanted to tell Shannon right away, but what if she hadn't gotten a part? Then Shannon called me. She was so excited that she could hardly talk. She and her twin sister, Molly, had both gotten parts, too. We couldn't wait to start working on the play together.

At the first rehearsal, we got our roles, and the whole cast read through the play together. I got the part of Pingle the 'Stute Fish in "How the Whale Got Its Throat." That's one of my favorite *Just So* stories.

There are 43 kids in the cast. Some kids have been in 10 or 12 productions, but a lot of them, like Shannon and Molly, have never been in a play before. Shannon is the crocodile in the story "How the Elephant Got Its Trunk," and Molly is the zebra in the story "How the Leopard Got Its Spots."

We got our rehearsal schedules after the first read-through. Rehearsal was scheduled for all day on Saturdays and after school until six o'clock every day except Monday. Since we had only four weeks until opening night, we knew we'd have to work hard.

On my way home from our first rehearsal, I checked out *Just So Stories* from the library. I read the whale story to my little sister, Caitlin, who is five. She can't wait until she's eight and old enough to try out for a play at the Children's Theatre.

The first time we rehearsed the whale story together,
we worked in Pat's office. We talked about the story,
and she asked us what we thought our characters were
like. I think Pingle is very smart because she always
tells the whale what to do. She's also a little sneaky.

We started each rehearsal with exercises called Basic
Eight. They're just like the stretching exercises we do
in school at the beginning of gym class. We have to
warm up our muscles because we use our whole bodies
when we act.

After the first week of rehearsals, Pat gave us
directions about where to move onstage. This is called
blocking. I wrote Pat's instructions down next to my
lines in the script so I could learn the blocking as I
memorized my lines.

There are three boys in the whale story with me.
Kevin and Dawson both play Smiler, the whale. They
wear a two-person costume and take turns being in
front. Jonathan is the shipwrecked mariner, Mr. Henry
Albert Bivvens, A.B. He gets eaten by Smiler, but he
gives the whale such a stomachache that Smiler
spits him back up.

The 'Stute Fish is the very last fish in the sea because
Smiler has eaten all the others. I swim just behind
Smiler's right ear so he won't eat me, too. When Smiler
says he's hungry, I tell him that man tastes nice. "Nice.
Nice but nubbly." That's my favorite line.

At each rehearsal, Pat wrote down her ideas about costumes, lighting, and developing the characters. She also timed each scene with a stopwatch so she would know exactly how long the show would be. Sometimes she asked one of us to take notes for her when we weren't onstage.

Dawson, Kevin, and I start our scene in the center of the stage. We swim upstage to find the shipwrecked mariner. It's easy for us to remember that upstage is toward the back of the stage because we go up the platforms to get there. Then we swim downstage with the mariner in the whale's stomach.

One of the things I had to practice was how to move like a fish. I also had to think about Pingle's personality and her voice. It's not easy being a fish! I worked on moving my arms like fins so that I would look and move like a real fish when I wore my costume.

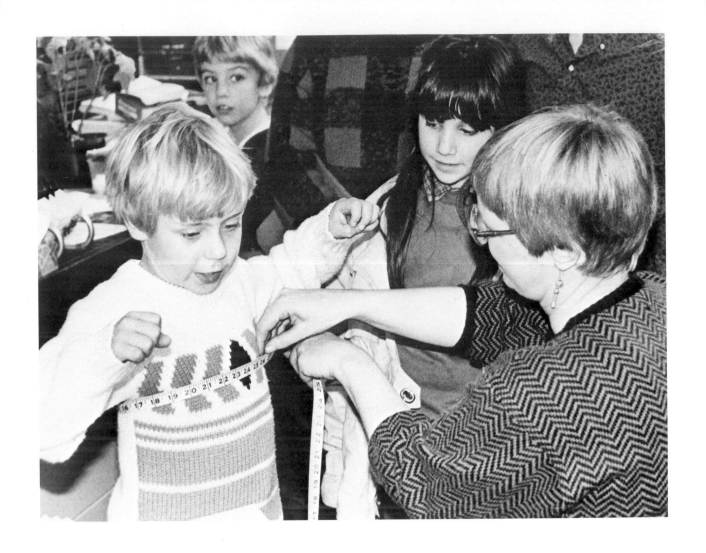

Sometimes when I wasn't rehearsing I helped Alison
downstairs in the costume shop. Alison Williams is
the theater's costume designer. She started measuring
us for costumes on the first day of rehearsals. She
showed me some sketches she had done at the zoo. She
says that if she can draw an animal and watch the
way it moves, she can build a costume that will look
like that animal.

I love to look at the thousands and thousands of costumes at the theater. About half of the costumes for our play were pulled from stock. They have been used in other plays and will be used again. The rest of our costumes had to be specially made for our play.

All the kids pitched in to help make the costumes.
Some of the sewing was done by hand and some was
done by machine.

   Jim Wallis is the designer and technical director
at the Children's Theatre. He and Pat planned all the
technical parts of the show such as scenery, sound,
and lighting. Then Jim figured out how to make their
ideas work onstage. He showed David how to install
metal rings called grommets into fabric so we could
paint it and hang it as part of the scenery.

Jim helped the kids on the stage crew build the set.
Just So Stories has a simple set, but even a simple
set takes a lot of work to make.

The kids on the stage crew did most of the technical
work, but the cast was expected to help whenever
we could. I moved the lighting instruments to where
they would be needed for the play. Shannon and Molly
both helped with this, too. I'd never used a wrench before. I found out that working with tools is a lot of fun.

Katharine is the propmaster for *Just So Stories*. She
is in charge of everything the cast carries or uses
onstage. She keeps all the props on the prop table
backstage in the order that we use them in the play.
That way, it's easy to find each prop as it's needed.

Brendan is working the lights for the show, and Scott is in charge of the sound effects. They both sit in the control booth at the back of the house. During the whale story, Scott plays a recording of a sea chanty whenever we are swimming around in the ocean.

We had our dress parade when all the costumes were
nearly finished. We modeled our costumes onstage for
Pat and Alison so they could see what the costumes
looked like and how they worked together in each scene.

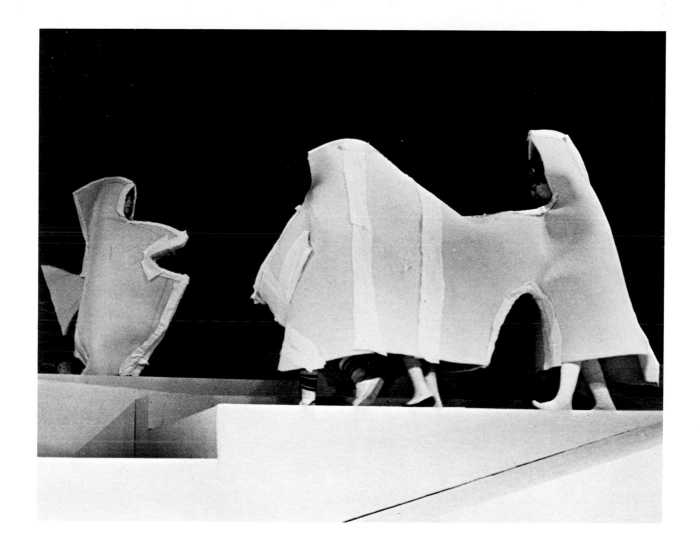

The costumes for the whale story weren't finished in
time for the dress parade. All we had to wear was gray
foam rubber held together with tape. It looked ugly, and
we kept tripping over it, but Pat didn't care what we
looked like at the dress parade. All she really wanted
to see was whether or not Jonathan could fit inside the
whale's mouth!

Alison gave us our finished costumes at the beginning of the first dress rehearsal. That's when we rehearse in full costume. Everyone wears ballet shoes during the play. It took me half an hour to find a pair that fit me.

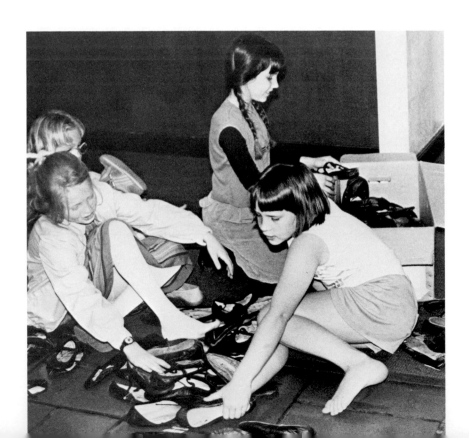

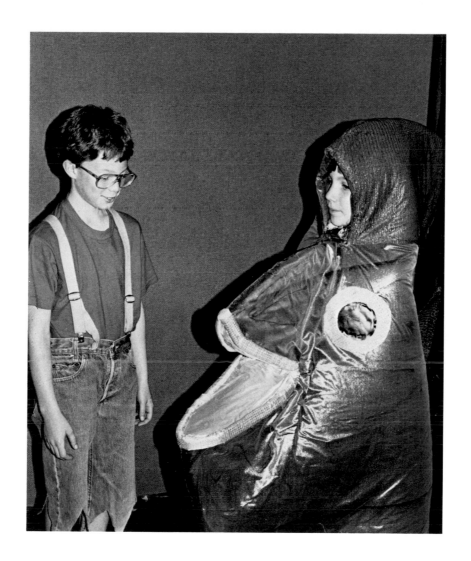

I was so happy when I saw my finished costume.
The rubber and tape were completely covered by
a beautiful, shiny red material.

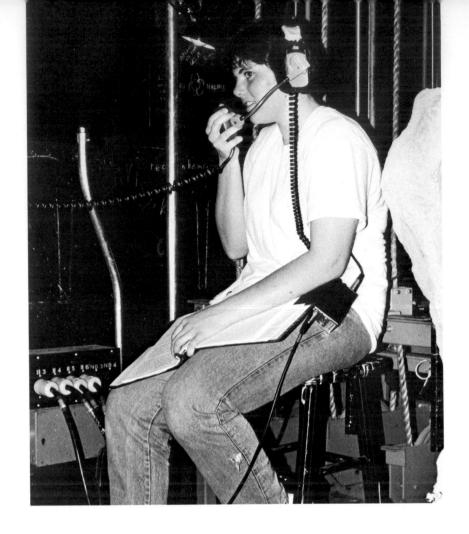

After spending so much time together, we all feel like one big family. I like to tease Maria, our stage manager, about being our mother because she's always telling us to be quiet backstage. Maria is 15. Once performances begin, she will be in charge of the whole production. During our dress rehearsals, she sat in the wings—backstage—and gave all the technical cues, or signals, just like she will do during each performance. The show begins when she cues Brendan to dim the house lights. She has to know the whole play by heart. If someone is sick for a performance, she may have to take over the part. She told me I'd better not get sick because my fish costume is too small for her.

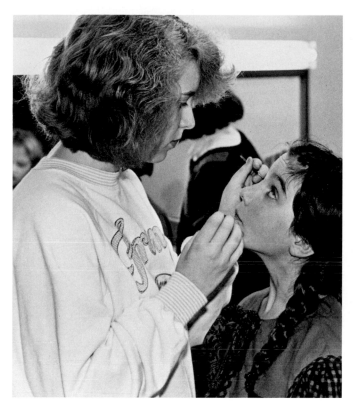

After four weeks of rehearsing and building the set, we're ready for our first performance tonight.

The first thing I did when I got to the theater today was put on my makeup. The eyeliner is the hardest part for me. Elena, who plays Mother Jaguar in "The Beginning of Armadillos," put my eyeliner on for me. She helped Shannon, too.

Once the whole cast was in costume, we sang the
Children's Theatre theme song and did a dance that
the older kids taught us. We chanted "good show"
faster and faster and louder and louder. After that,
I felt ready to be Pingle the 'Stute Fish.

When we were all backstage, we heard someone say "the house is open." I knew I had to be very quiet then because the house manager had started letting the audience in. My parents and my sister are coming to the performance tonight. All 200 tickets have been sold. We have a full house.

Right now, I have butterflies in my stomach. What if I forget all my lines? But once I get onstage and begin acting, I know I'll forget about being scared.

The stories in our performance are narrated by the
Beings, who are magicians and genies. The play begins
when the Eldest Magician takes the Beings back to
"when the world was so new-and-all."

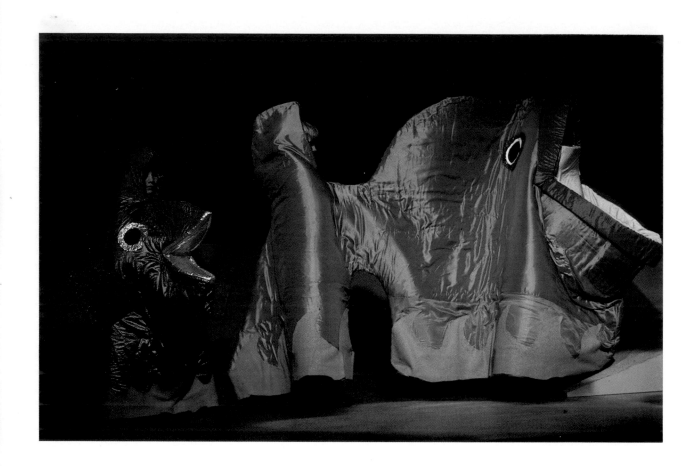

Waiting to go onstage is hard, but at last it's time
for our story. As soon as the audience sees our costumes,
they applaud. We have to wait until the house is quiet
before Smiler says he is hungry. I tell him to swim to
latitude Fifty North, longitude Forty West, where he'll
find a shipwrecked mariner sitting on a raft. I warn
him that the mariner is a man of "infinite-resource-
and-sagacity."

But Smiler swallows the mariner anyway—raft, jack-knife, suspenders, and all. Inside the whale, the mariner jumps so hard that he gives Smiler the hiccoughs.

Smiler soon decides that man is too "nubbly" and
wants to spit the mariner out. But the mariner won't
come out until the whale takes him home.

On the journey back to his home, the mariner whittles his raft into a grate. When the mariner reaches home, he ties the grate into the whale's throat with his suspenders so that the whale can't eat anything but very, very small fish. When I see what's happening, I quietly swim away.

When the play is over, the audience begins to
applaud, and all of us come back onstage for curtain
call. I think the audience had as much fun as we did.

After every performance at the Children's Theatre,
the cast goes into the lobby to meet the audience.
When we went into the lobby, I got to meet Patty
McEwen. She was in the very first play at the
Children's Theatre.

I love it when the little kids in the audience ask me
to sign their programs, but this time I couldn't sign
any programs or even hold the flowers my parents
and Caitlin brought me because my arms were inside
the fish's mouth.

Now that opening night is over, the cast and crew are going out for ice cream. Most of us didn't even know each other when we tried out for the play, but now we're all good friends. It's fun to sit around and talk about our first show. We're going to put on six more performances of *Just So Stories*. We'll try to make each performance as special as opening night.

Right after the last performance, we'll strike the set. After each production, everything used in the play has to be put away. Everyone has a job to do during strike.

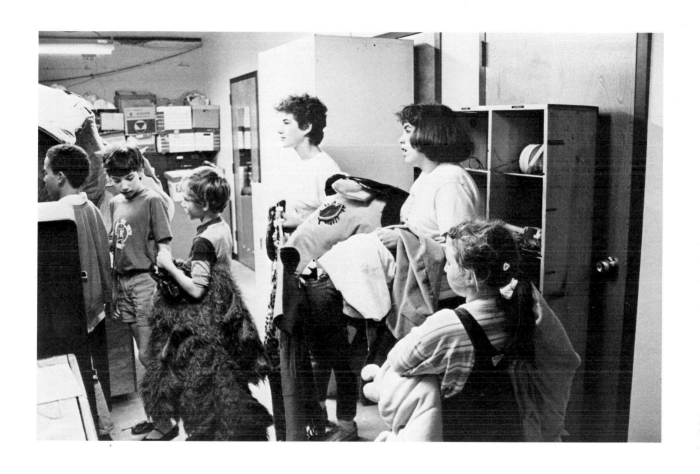

All of the costumes will be taken back to the costume
room and put away.

The props will all go back into storage in the prop room, which is underneath the stage.

We'll have to take down the painted fabric we used
for the scenery. Then the platforms will have to be
taken apart and stored in the flat house. That's where
the sets are kept.

It's a tradition at the Children's Theatre to sign
your name and the name of your play on the shop wall.
Kids have been doing it for so long that it's hard to
find an empty spot. Shannon and I want to find a place
where we can sign our names together.

Strike is such a busy time. It's also a sad time because it means the end of another production. After strike, the stage always looks empty. But tryouts for the next play will begin soon after we strike the set for *Just So Stories*.

I want to try out for the next play, too. It's hard
work, but being part of a play is a lot of fun, onstage
and backstage.